Beauty from Ashes

Mindy Jones

BookLeaf Publishing

India | USA | UK

Presentation by *BookLeaf Publishing*

Web: www.bookleafpub.com

E-mail: info@bookleafpub.com

ISBN: 9789360947941

First edition 2024

*For my children, Vivian and Sid Jr. - I pray
you will always know how very much you
are loved.*

*Beloved - you were the spark that set it all
ablaze.*

ACKNOWLEDGEMENT

First and foremost, I thank God, the source of my inspiration, creativity, and strength. Your Love and Presence have been my constant in life's journey and this book's creation.

Thank you to Sid, Misty, my parents, and my amazing family for your unwavering love and support. Your belief in me has been a beacon through my darkest times and a celebration in my brightest.

Thank you, Mollie, my dearest friend. There just isn't enough space to express all my gratitude.

To the ones who have always pointed me back to the One who can calm my spirit and silence my fears, thank you.

A special thanks to Catherine and Jodie for providing the space for me to find my way through some of the darkest moments of my life without judgment. Instead of telling me what I should or shouldn't do, you both helped me find the courage to look within and discover that the answers were within me all along; I just needed to listen.

To the poetry community on Instagram, thank you for providing a space where words can dance freely and voices like mine can be heard. Your encouragement and feedback have been invaluable.

Lastly, to you, dear reader, for picking up this book and joining me on this journey. This collection is my story and reflects the universal journey of self-discovery, love, loss, and rebirth. Thank you for allowing my words into your world.

With deepest appreciation,
Mindy Jones

PREFACE

Dear Reader,

Welcome to a journey through the verses of "Beauty from Ashes." This book, a labor of love and a voyage into the depths of the soul, is my heart laid bare on paper. Each poem here is a piece of my journey, a fragment of my transformation, as I navigated the complex terrains of love, loss, grief, and self-discovery.

In these pages, you will find poems that speak of the fiery trials of love, the ashes of heartbreak, and the beauty of rising anew. I have penned these verses not only as a testament to my own journey but as a beacon for anyone who has ever felt lost in the wilderness of their emotions and self-discovery. It is for those who have braved the flames of passion, have been scarred, yet have found the strength to rise again.

This collection is a celebration of the human spirit's resilience. Like a phoenix, we, too, can emerge stronger and more beautiful from our trials. These poems are an invitation to embrace your own rebirth, find your voice amidst the echoes of your experiences, and see the beauty in your own ashes.

As you turn these pages, I hope your own story resonates with the words and emotions contained within. May this book be a companion to you on your journey towards self-discovery, a guide as you navigate the intricate paths of love, and a reminder that from the ashes of our experiences, we can rise with newfound beauty and strength.

With love and light,
Mindy Jones

A Lovely Mask

Long length.
Eyes staring back at me.
I know you.
I've seen your face before.
But your eyes.
Something has changed.
They see beyond my frame.
Peering inside with Spirit's eyes, dividing soul
from spirit, bone from marrow.
You see me and interpret my true thoughts.
Bringing the secret motives of my heart out to be
laid bare.
All
for the world
to see.
And it sees me.
I am naked. I have no walls to cling to.
Nor do I want to.

No place to hide, so I stare back.
You see me.
     Know me.
        Love me.
In all my weaknesses and shortcomings.
My
    faults
    failures
          You see what lies beneath.
And it's not pretty.
A dark mass.
A cesspool of sin.
Locked away, in hopes of hiding it there forever.
I thought if I could lock it up, it would behave.
Hiding the dark side on my finest days.
It was a lovely mask.
Some might say.
But you knew.
You always knew.

The Real Prisoner

Who is this prisoner?
She who roams the corridors of my heart.
Down the long winding path of doors that lead
to rooms, locked from the outside.
Or are they?

Does the ring of keys jingle from her wrist?
Does she taunt me?
Threatening to unlock one?
Is she waiting for the perfect time to let the
perfect one out?

I see her.
White flowing gown.
Running her fingertips along the wall.
                         along the doors
Listening.
      Sensing.

Studying my every move
            every thought
            every desire

She knows the perfect moment to open the
perfect door.

"You can come this close and no further."
She says that to me
                to everyone.

Sometimes she gives me years.
Years to get comfortable
        to feel safe
        to feel loved
                needed
                wanted

There goes the insertion of the key
            the turning of the lock
            the twisting of the knob
            the pulling of the door
I know that sound
        the sound of my door
                    my knob
            my lock
                        my key
    my room
                my cell

My hell

Will the real Mindy
please
come
forward?

She Longs to Sing

I don't know who I am
Or where I am going.
In a world so vast
Yet intimately knowing.
Through streets uncharted
Under skies wide and open
I seek words unspoken
Truths yet unbroken.

Through every step
In time and space
Fragments I find
In the world's embrace.
And with the dawn's gentle caress
And twilight's soft farewell
I journey through the unknown
In a story, mine to tell.

In the laughter of the stream
And the wisdom of the trees
In every leaf's gentle sway
I find parts of me.
In this endless search
Not for fame or worldly things
But for the song within my heart
That she longs to sing.

Missing Pieces

Wandering through memories
Each is a faded song.
I believe that where I'm going
Is where I belong.
In the journey through the shadows
In the breaking of the dawn
I found all the missing pieces
That I thought were long gone.

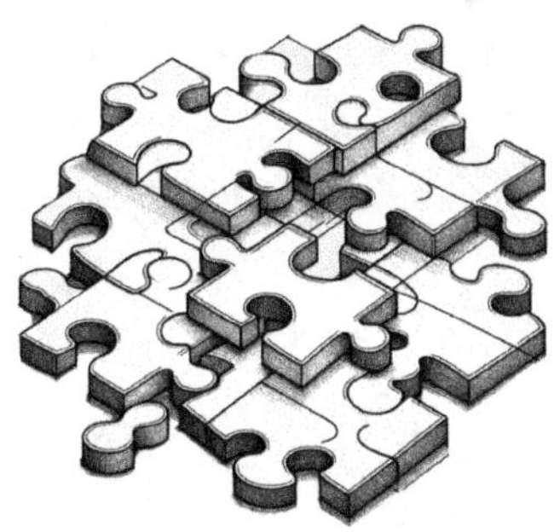

Places I Hide

My song whispers secrets
Of my essence in a frame.
It's the colorful silence
That calls out my name.

Have you heard the notes
That pull my heart's strings
With melodies that speak
In the songs that I sing?

A hidden part within
Awakens unaware.
In every chord and verse
I lay myself bare.

Vibrations of sound
Mirror what's deep inside
Revealing the depths
Of the places I hide.

Embrace Yourself

In your flaws there is beauty to see,
Your collection of experiences is what makes
you unique.
With each step, in love, you grow,
Embrace yourself and let your light show.

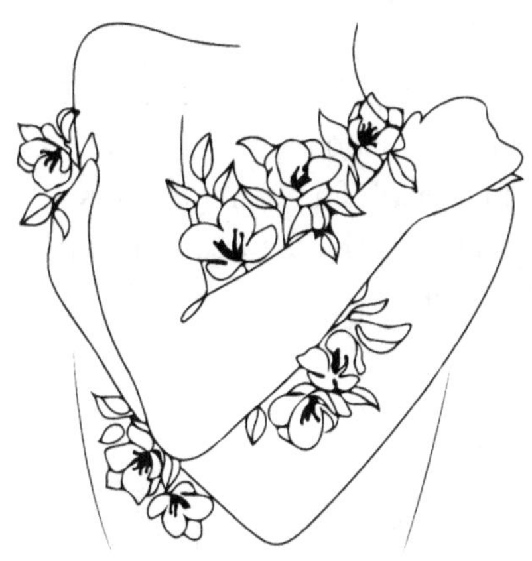

Geography of My Soul

I thought I was ok
Standing alone in a room painted
In shades of my own resilience
Mirror reflecting a replica of courage.

But a crack appeared
Not in the glass but behind my eyes
A fissure in the well-worn narrative
I spun for self-comfort.

I've come to recognize that I am not a lone wolf,
wandering in isolation;
Instead, I am part of a greater tapestry,
woven together with the threads of community
and connection.

Traumas, joys, and insecurities
all demand a voice.

So I listen
Not just to the easy melodies
Of self-praise and external validation,
But to the discordant chords
That play the complex symphony
In my internal world.

I am still not "ok"
And maybe that's the point
For in the raw space between "ok" and "not"
I discovered the geography of my soul
A land more honest, more flawed
And infinitely more beautiful
Than I ever dared to see.

You

Maybe it was me
And you were always right.
A mirror of my flaws
Exposed when touched by light.

Then, all the missing pieces
Of my heart collided with love
And suddenly, a garden grew
When light came from above.

Convinced, I held the ink
And that my truth meant more
I thought I had penned my story
Like all the times before.

Yet you were the steady hand
Guiding the whole way
The voice within my garden

Beckoning me to stay.

Unraveling my tangled mind
One
        flower
                at
                        a time.

A Reason to Sing

The song remains unsung
And the lyrics' unwritten
But the melody still exists.

Each inhale
A question.
Each exhale
An unknown.
But in the space between
I can hear her sing.

So I let go.

My lungs absorb a fog of uncertainties.
Each exhaled breath
Giving voice to the words
I could never say before.

With every breath
The atmosphere shifts
And the world receives
My unvoiced longings.

So, I hold my breath no longer.
For even in uncertainty
I find a reason to breathe.
I find a reason to sing.

Tend to Your Garden

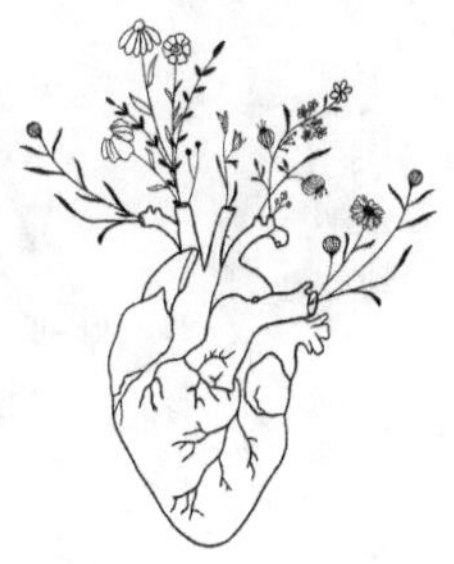

In the mirror of life, a reflection true
A story untold, the heart's deepest hue.
Gazing within, through layers unseen
Discovering love where shadows had been.

Embrace your scars and the tales they impart
For within those lines lies the art of your heart.
Each flaw, a chapter of your strength in disguise
A journey of learning beneath open skies.

Tend to your garden with kindness and care
Plant seeds of self-love in soil rich and fair.
Watch as they flourish in warmth and in light
Blossoming fully from morning till night.

Words

Some days
words flow effortlessly
from my pen
flawlessly falling onto paper.

Other days
they seep out of the cracks
of my brokenness
revealing fractures so sharp
that they cut paper
fingers
and lips.

Love and Ink

In the realm where ink and parchment dwell
She paints a story only few can tell.
With a pen that dances, gleaming gold,
On timeworn letters, tales of old.

Roses blush in hues of fire
Amidst whispered secrets of all her desires.
Watercolors bleed, this love, profound
Where memories and dreams are tightly bound.

The release of emotion, vivid and deep,
Where love and sorrow silently weep.
For in each stroke and in every line
Her heart and her soul forever entwine.

The Wilderness

The wilderness
Untamed and free
Where secrets are whispered
And my heart is set free.

In losing myself
Nothing is lost
A process of shedding
And counting the cost.

This path I'm on
A journey yet unknown
Many parts of me
Have yet to be shown

Stripping off masks
I so tirelessly wear
To hide my vulnerabilities
Raw and bare.

Out here is where I find Him
That Sacred Fire within
The holy longing for His Love
No longer be hidden.

Losing myself
To find where I might end
A release of my spirit
For new life to begin.

My Heart

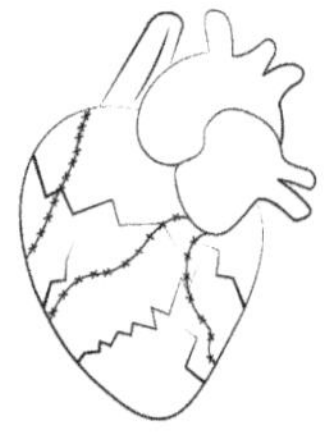

My heart knows my rhythm, soft and slow.
She whispers in beats, life's ebb and flow.
She dances beneath my cage of bone.
And in silent chambers, she sings alone.

She knows love's tender, fierce embrace.
Of wild joy and sorrow's haunting trace.
She keeps the secrets of my silent tears
And the dreams that have outlasted all of my
years.

In every throb, a story she tells
Of the battles I fought and where angels fell.
She remembers each promise ever spoken
And holds onto every word, each a token.

My heart knows the depths of every sea
The heights of my bliss, my agony.
She maps the journey of my days
In this pulsing life, in a myriad ways.

Alive

Days cascade like water drops.
Each one is a universe of possibility.
Another year to face the unknown.
Another chance to rewrite the script.

Will this be the year my pen stops trembling?
Will the words finally fall into place?
Will the rhythm finally find its groove?

Will this be the year my pen stops?

All the rush of impulsive leaps
Contribute to this unfinished work.

Only He knows when it's finished.

Another year, another question.
A blank canvas laid bare for the painting to
begin.
Will this be the year of brushstrokes filled with
joy and happiness or pain and sorrow?
Will this be a year filled with tortured strokes
that will all contribute to the building up or
tearing down of me?

Only He knows.

So I rest in Him.

Through it all, we collect fragments
Little pieces of what it means to be alive.
And as long as you're alive…
Be alive!

Solace

I found solace in music
Words calling forth the girl that I lost
Reminding her of what it was like to feel
And that numbing all her pain came at a cost.

I found a familiar friend
In how the music danced in my soul
Bringing me to life again
On the path to becoming whole.

How the rhythms called out to my heart
Reminding her how to beat
With sacred tempos of moving wonder
In songs I played on repeat.

I found solace in those moments
That took me deep within
To the inner recesses of my heart
Where I was born again.

Inside She Knows

Inside she knows, there's a strength that glows
A force unseen, like a river that flows.
In the quiet of night, when the world is at rest
She feels it stir, deep within her chest.

Her light flickers, in the darkest of times
A melody that plays in her intricate rhymes.
In the mirror, she gazes, through trials and pain
Understanding each scar, each loss, each gain.

With each challenge, her strength becomes more
clear
With whispers of courage, only she can hear.
He guides her steps, through paths untrod
A beacon of hope, a gift from God.

With a fire in her heart that never ceases to burn

Is a lesson she faces, with something to learn.
She's a warrior, a healer, in her own unique tale
With every fall and rise, she knows she won't
fail.

Inside she knows, as she faces each day
With her strength within, she'll find her way.
Through storms and sunshine, in laughter and
tears
Her inner voice will guide her, through the
years.

The Strong One

I was the strong one
I helped others find their missing parts.
But when I fell and broke my shell
Everyone seemed to depart.

My heart never mattered to them.

Serendipity

By happenstance, I met him.
Among the glass and crumbling stone.
My eyes locked into the gaze
Of a soul, I've always known.

A mirror reflecting mysteries
And secrets yet unknown.
He was the missing piece
In the puzzle of my soul.

My heart stirred
Hearing this forgotten song.
A melody buried in the chaos
Of my soul where he belonged.

And there we stood.
Two souls in a world come undone.
Among the discord and strife
We found unity where there was none.

Now, we sift through the ruins
He and I, hand in hand.
Finding pieces long scattered
Though no one understands.

As serendipity would have it
Fate had its final say.
Our ruins become the temple
Where love and new dreams lay.

Presence

You surprised me with the joy of your presence.
I wasn't looking for you.
I didn't know how much I needed you.

You are oxygen.
I didn't know I couldn't breathe.
You are nourishment.
I didn't know I was starving.
You are water.
I didn't know I was thirsty.
You are light.
I didn't know I was in darkness.

You are…
        everything.

Evanescence

The evanescent moments we share
Hang in the air like incense.
I just want to be with you
Lost in the fragrance of your love.
So intoxicating is your scent.

I am captivated
By the melodies that you create
When you speak.
Notes cascade from your voice
Like raindrops from the sky.
Each one contains a world
                    an emotion
                    a prayer.

I am captivated by your words
Written on paper
Sentences that give shape
To the formless.
Each phrase is a fragment
Of a larger narrative.

I write it all down
Each word is an anchor
In the turbulent sea of existence.

A pause—
A momentary lapse in the continuum
As you look me in the eyes.
Perfection.

Inner healing threads
Our conversations.
You are a gentle river
Cradling broken stones
Smoothing edges
Filling cracks.

Your voice
A balm
Your words
Stepping stones
In a stream of consciousness.

You are a sanctuary
Of love and understanding
Where the fragmented pieces
Of myself are embraced
                acknowledged
                and made whole.

We talk of God
And of Jesus
Exploring corridors of belief
As if wandering

In a maze of mirrors
With each reflection
Revealing another facet of truth.

And we let it be –
Floating in the evanescent
Embracing the ephemeral.
Because even if the moments pass
Their echoes remain—
Indelible imprints on our souls
Written not in ink
But in the language of being.

Exposed

I let you in
to a place so secret
and so primal.

Now fear
is clawing at me…
    screaming at me…
  warning me of danger.

My heart's been exposed…
    and now…
  you hold it in your hands.

You could crush it
and I would be broken…

forever.
You could cherish it,
and I would be yours…
    forever.

Tell me…
What will you do
with what I have given you?

Battleground

I'm afraid of him.
For beneath the allure
lies a complexity I can't fully grasp.

His intensity casts a spell.
Yet, within that spell
are shadows I dare not explore.

Like a flame, he draws me near.
But I fear the inevitable burn.

My mind is a battleground
of desire and caution.
Urging me to step closer
yet warning me to retreat.

It's this paradox
that keeps me shivering.
Caught between wanting to know him
and fearing what I might discover.

Shared Fantasy

I'm lost in your gaze.
An invisible gravity, pulling on my heartstrings.
Leaving trails of stardust.
A secret path to where only we exist.

You bring melody to my chaos,
Echoing in the chambers of my soul,
Every note is a brushstroke on my canvas,
Painting feelings too vast for words.

In your eyes, galaxies unfold
a universe of possibilities.
Time ceases to rush by,
and every moment is a cataclysmic event.

Love is not a fleeting whisper,
but a thunderous declaration,
resounding through the spaces between stars,
illuminating the dark corners of my being.

I'm anchored in your embrace
yet free to explore the depths of this love.
A paradox, as enigmatic as the night sky.
Every touch, a constellation to discover.

You are the gravity that grounds me,
Yet the force that propels me to soar,
In this dance of light and shadow,
I am in love, completely, unreservedly.

Is this your fantasy?
Or mine.

She Deserves

She deserves the universe
and all its boundless wonders;
she wants the chorus,
not mere echoes of love
to keep her satisfied.

No crumb of affection shall satisfy;
only a banquet of genuine,
unwavering devotion will do.

She refuses to dance
to the rhythm of another's time.
Instead, she moves to the beat
of her heart's own song.

If you are graced with the warmth
of her affection,
let your actions resonate with
a worthiness that mirrors her own.

For she holds the moon and the stars
and the whole galaxy
within the universe of her soul,
and she'll no longer share it
with those who cannot fathom its depths,
nor cherish its boundless wonder.

I Am Yours

I am yours, in every whisper of the dawn,
In quiet moments when the world is withdrawn.
In every gentle touch of rain,
In joyous heights and depths of pain.
I am yours.

I am yours, where melodies entwine,
In the silent language of you and I.
In every star that graces night,
And in the dawn's first gentle light.
I am yours.

I am yours, in twilight's embrace,
In the subtle shifts of time and space.
In every dream where you appear,
In every hope, in every fear.
I am yours.

Accepted

He embraces every part of me
He loves each one the same.
And when I fear that I'm too dark to love
He softly speaks my name.

He tells me he delights in me
And he listens to my cries.
He turns my chaos into melodies
When I'm lost in his eyes.

For in his eyes, I find a home
My sanctuary of grace.
He shows me love I've never known
In his arms, I find my place.

Little Castle

When I shut down and become
A labyrinth all to myself
He doesn't seek to solve me.
Instead, he walks the maze by my side.
He knows I get lost
Inside my little castle
And he waits.
Silently.
Patiently.
Loving me.
Until I'm brave enough
To come out again.

Love and Thorns

In my garden, love and sorrow meet,
Beneath the sun's relentless heat,
There's a rose, both gentle and divine,
Around its stem, sharp thorns entwine.

Her petals soft as whispered dreams,
Glistening with morning's dewy gleams,
Yet beneath her beauty, so serene,
Lies a caution that is not easily seen.

For every heart that seeks to hold,
Her bloom of love, fierce and bold,
Must brave the piercing thorns of trial,
A journey long, yet worth the while.

Thorns of fear, and doubt, and pain,
Guard her love that one hopes to gain.
Each prick a lesson, a test, to see,
If your heart can align in true harmony.

In the embrace of thorns, love is found,
Not in ease, but where challenges abound.
For only through trials, tough and sore,
Does the heart grow stronger, loving more.

Through pain and joy, a path is worn,
In her garden, where true love is born.
So hold her close with all her thorns,
For love, true love, is forevermore.

Our Dance of Love

In the garden of my heart, love blooms bright,
A tender vine, growing through the night.
It whispers soft in the moon's gentle glow,
In its embrace, the true selves we show.

With petals of trust, and thorns of fear,
Love is a journey, that draws our souls near.
In its depth, a world, vast and profound,
Where the whispers of passion and dreams are
found.

In our dance of love, our two hearts entwine,
Sharing whispers, like vintage wine.
Through storms and calm, our love stands,
unswayed,
A lighthouse guiding, when we're afraid.

In love's soft light, shadows flee away,
Revealing our hearts in the bright of day.
It's a melody, sung in two parts,
A symphony played in the garden of my heart.

Every Moment With You

Every moment with you has illuminated my
world
in ways I never thought possible.
Your love is like a gentle sunrise
after a long night, a symphony that fills the
silent spaces of my heart.

It's a kind of magic that turns ordinary moments
into unforgettable memories.
With you, I've felt the deepest joys
and discovered parts of myself I never knew
existed.

Your love is a wonderful gift,
one I cherish every day.
It's more than just a feeling;
it's a force that has transformed my life
in the most beautiful ways.

You Became the Fire in Me

You became the fire in me.
Your spark set me aflame.
With passion's breath,
you fanned the flame,
gave strength to love,
I dare not tame.

The Elements

Wind
He was the wind
that swept me away,
with just a whisper of my name.
And all my walls went too.

Wildfire
You saw that I was cold
So you set my heart aflame.
*How could you have known that a wildfire would
break out?*

Sunshine
Love and pain
Sunshine and rain
Why can't I bottle sun rays like you bottle up my
tears?
Then I could save it for a rainy day.

Dirt
I found you on the road,
paved with sludge and bones.
No light to guide my way,
No lamp upon the stones.

Rain

Let the rain sing; let her cleanse and revive,
Let her send a rainbow that makes our spirits
thrive.
In every raindrop, refreshing is found,
in every color, there is beauty all around.

Words Like Fireflies

He whispers words like fireflies,
Igniting paths I've never seen.
He leads me through the underbrush,
To places I've never been.

Silence and Love Speak

In every subtle nuance,
our storyline unfolds,
As if our souls are writing in invisible ink.
In every tender moment,
where our dreams dare to meet,
We find a hidden language,
where silence and love speak.

I Am Captivated

You echo my favorite pastime,
like the final note in my life's symphony.

Like a melody that resonates within,
you harmonize the chaos,
bringing a sense of peace and completeness.

With you, every one of my endings
is transformed into a gateway to new
beginnings.

You hold the key, unlocking the most beautiful
chapter.
Opening doors to realms of beauty
and wonder that I never knew existed.
And I am captivated.

I Am His

I am his and he is mine,
In every star, his love does shine.
Boundless, endless, like the sea,
His grace unfolds to set my soul free.

In whispered winds, his voice I hear,
A symphony, so sweet, a sound, so clear.
Through storms and calm, in light and dark,
His presence is my guiding ark.

In blooming fields, his touch I feel,
A love so deep, so true, so real.
He paints my days in shades of grace,
In every line, his love I trace.

He is the sun, the moon, the sky,
In every tear, in every sigh.

Through trials and joys, in love's great dance,
In him, I find my true expanse.

So, I am his, forevermore,
A journey to an unseen shore.
In every beat, in every line,
Eternally his, and his heart is mine.

All of Me

Gentle at first
You drew me near.
With promises
Only I could hear.
A mask so perfect
It fooled even me
Blinded by love
I couldn't see.

I woke up
In a fog so deep.
A nightmare had stirred
In love's lost sleep.
My sense of self
Fractured, but there.
With gentle grace
I will repair.

You remain a whisper.
A hard lesson learned.
A page that I've turned
But cannot seem to burn.
And as I mend
My heart is set free.
And as the veil lifts
I see all of me.

Tell Me

Tell me that love is enough, to light the darkest
path.
Tell me that it is enough, to give it all we have.
Tell me that love is enough, to heal the deepest
scars.
Tell me that it is enough, to heal even ours.

Tell me that love is enough, to weather every
storm,
Tell me it's like a fire, there to keep us warm.
Tell me that love is enough, to bridge every
divide,
To unify our souls, with nothing to hide.

Tell me that our love is enough, and I'll believe
it's true.
For all of my life, I so wanted it to be you.

Will You Still Think of Me?

Will you still think of me,
when the stars have faded from your sky,
when the melodies of our shared days
dissolve into the quiet hum of the night?

In the hush of the twilight hours,
as the world softens its edges,
will your thoughts wander,
like lost birds, to the nest of our memories?

Will you remember the laughter,
spilling like sunlight through old windows,
the way our words danced,
a delicate ballet of understanding and whimsy?

In the solitude of your journey,
through the forests of your dreams,
will my voice echo,
a distant yet familiar song?

Will you still think of me,
when the rain whispers secrets on your
windowpane,
and the wind carries tales
of a love that bloomed in the silence of being?

As seasons shift and years unfold,
like pages in a well-loved book,
will our story rest in your heart,
a soft glow in the twilight of your thoughts?

Love Must Flow Free

I shared you with no one, because I knew,
That no one would understand, the love between
me and you.
What we had was sacred, so pure and so rare,
And it was a secret, that we alone could bear.

We shared our hopes and our dreams, and even
our past hurts.
And the times we've felt the most alone,
with no strength left to exert.

In the garden where only we could tread,
And every word that we left unsaid,
We nurtured blooms of love with roots so deep,
That no one could harm, if we ever fell asleep.

But in our seclusion, we found the cost,
In keeping you close, something was lost.
For love, like a river, it must flow free,
Not hidden in shadows, with just you and me.

And now I am learning, that love's truest grace,
Lies not in seclusion, but in open space,
Where our hearts, unguarded, can truly soar,
Where in sharing our love, it would grow ever
more.

I want to share you, not with fear, but with pride,
For love is a journey, not a place to hide.
In the open, our love will find its truest part,
And in the sharing, your heart would become my
heart.

I hope it's not too late.

What Happened?

What happened to the dreams we sowed,
In fields of hope, where once they glowed?
Lost in the maze of life's grand play,
Where shadows loom and skies turn grey.

When did the laughter softly fade,
in the forest of memories that we made?
Echoes of joy, now whisper light,
Dancing away, like birds in flight.

What happened to the words we left unsaid,
The silent thoughts inside our head?
Gentle murmurs of heart's desire,

Quenched too soon, like fleeting fire.

In the quiet of the night's embrace,
In the tender hush of this sacred space,
Our dreams, our laughter, and words unsaid,
Live on within…
not lost…
not dead…

For what happened to us is not an end,
But a curve along the path we bend.
In every dusk, a dawn is born,
In every tear, hope is reborn.
So, what happened to us is just a pause,
In life's relentless, beautiful cause.
A chance to breathe, to love, to see,
What happened to us is a part of you and me.

We Create Melodies

Together we create melodies so rare,
A symphony of love, beyond compare.
Your heart whispers of wisdom and tales,
And mine sings of dreams that I know will never
fail.

You Are The Melody

You are the melody in every song I sing,
the harmony to which my soul clings.
And in quiet moments, when words depart,
the silence speaks that you have my heart.

The Sacred Flame of Memory

Here again…
silence burns your memory into a symphony of
whispers.
Each note a gentle caress
upon my soul's skin.

Time, the thief, returns the jewels of moments
past,
casting them like stars across the veil of my
thoughts.

In this quiet, your laughter echoes,
a serenade amidst the stillness, unforgotten, so
dear.
The shadows dance to the rhythm of your being,
drawing me into the waltz of yesteryears.

The fragrance of lost days lingers,
a bouquet of dreams undimmed by the sun's
march.
Here in the hush, where heartbeats speak,
your memory, a sacred flame, flickers—never to
be undone.

The Space Between

I'm in the space between loving you or me, if I
let you go will it set my heart free?
If I give up the hold that I have on tomorrow,
will you find me in joy, will you meet me in
sorrow?

I hear the song that we used to sing, but to the
notes I can no longer cling.
It's all been sung before, now it's me lying on
the floor.

We Touched the Sky

In a room with walls of passion, we made a
home,
Love the foundation, on which all else was
sown.
Yet, beneath the hearth where flames once
brightly danced,
Lies the unspoken truth, leaving both of us
entranced.

Love, a fervent fire, but not a mason skilled,
Can spark a world of dreams, yet leave them
unfulfilled.
It sings in dulcet tones, but lacks a solid word,
To solve the puzzles raw, and stories still
unheard.

We touched the sky, but could not grasp a star,
Lost in the dance of love, forgetting who we are.
Woven in a tapestry of laughter, tears, and touch,
But threads of understanding missed, and needed
much.

The ink of love writes bold, but can't complete
the tale,
When chapters of reality are heavy, hard, and
frail.

Though love, a potent spell, it's not the only key,
To open doors of joy and peace, and shared
eternity.

So here we stand, at crossroads, parting ways,
enough—
A lesson learned is that love alone is simply not
enough.

We touched the sky, but couldn't grasp the stars.
Love alone was not enough, to heal all these
scars.
And beneath the hearth where flames once
brightly danced,
Lies the unspoken truth, that we never had a
chance.

The Life in Me

The seasons shifted,
and the winds, they changed.
Our paths diverged
as our lives rearranged.

Yet in my being,
he forever will be,
the air, the pulse, the life in me.

I Wish You Were Mine

I've tried to walk away so many times
But just one look and all my walls
go crumbling to the ground.

You reach out your hand,
and like a magnet,
I'm pulled right back into you.

Your love is intoxicating,
sending every chemical swirling
throughout every cell in my body.
There is no place I can go
where you are not.

Silence hauntingly announces
your absence.
Emptiness presses firmly
against my skin.
Reminding me of what your body
felt like against mine.

Your scent lingers,
sending a chill to my core.
Reminding me, I am yours.

How I wish that you were mine.

How Did I Get Here?

My longing for you has led me to this place.
It was never enough just to be satisfied.
One taste of your love and I was undone.
One glimpse of your beauty and my heart was
ravished.

I have never seen such beauty.
Never felt such pain for more of anything in my
life.

The flame of your love set me on fire.
And all I want to do is
 Burn…
 Burn…
 Burn…
Until all that is left are the ashes
of my once-beating heart
that caught the tempo of your love.

How could I go back?
How could I ever go back?
I cannot unsee you…
        unknow you…

I cannot forget your voice…
 your face…

your touch…
your love…

Where did you go?

You have left me here alone
to fend for myself.
Where are you?

You did this to me.
You led me to this place.

Your Touch

Your touch lingers on my skin.
Your ghost echoes deep within.
Every place you touched now aches,
with whispers of your presence.
Seared in my memory,
an indelible imprint that scorches my thoughts
with a bittersweet intensity.

The Come Down

It's the come down now.
No rush of chemicals
from your intoxicating touch.
The world, once vibrant,
fades into sepia and gray.

The words that remained
echoing in my mind,
now dissolving into
the quiet morning light.

In this stillness, I go inward,
Where memories of you
dance like shadows.
Fleeting, yet etched deep
in my heart's canvas.

Whispers of your voice
hum an eerie tune.
It lingers…
a hauntingly sweet melody.

Love's embrace has loosened,
Leaving behind death and destruction.
The death of me.
The death of you.

The death of us.

An empty space beside me,
filled only with echoes
of a love that burned bright,
then gently faded.

Even in loss, beauty remains.
A soft glow lingers in your absence.
So I carry with me the soft afterglow,
of a love that once set my soul ablaze.

Untitled

I've become the poem
you never wanted to write.
The song you never wanted to sing.

What will the title be?

You Are More

You are more than shattered art,
Each piece a shard of your broken heart.
Stand up, you've known this all before,
Don't stay broken on the floor.

He's not worth it.

She is Broken

I could pretend I wasn't broken
But that would be a lie.
The truth is, I need some space
To let my heart just cry.
She
       Is
              Broken

Fortress

My heart turned silent and lifted her walls,
A fortress of solitude, echoes, and halls.
But even the sternest of walls do confess,
In the silence they hold, my heart nonetheless.

For hearts that bear the cruelest blow,
Are those who learn, heal, and grow.
And in the end, what's true will stand,
A love that's kind, with a gentle hand.

Broken Becomes Whole

Rain falls to cover my tears.
A delicate dance, an embrace of fears.
Each droplet sings a sorrowful song.
A tune where grief and grace belong.

Thunder roars its defiant cry,
As lightning scars the blackened sky.
Yet, within the storm, a tranquil plea,
A call for love, for you and me.

The winds whisper secrets old,
Of heroes lost and stories untold.
They carry your voice, a comforting tone,
A reminder that I'm never truly alone.

In the tempest, my spirit, finds its way,
A compass of hope on a clouded day.
And as the rain melds with my tears,
I find a peace that outshines my fears.

So let it pour, let the heavens weep,
For rain has promises it's sworn to keep.
In every drop, a mirror to my soul,
A liquid prism, where broken, becomes whole.

Lessons from Dirt and Dust

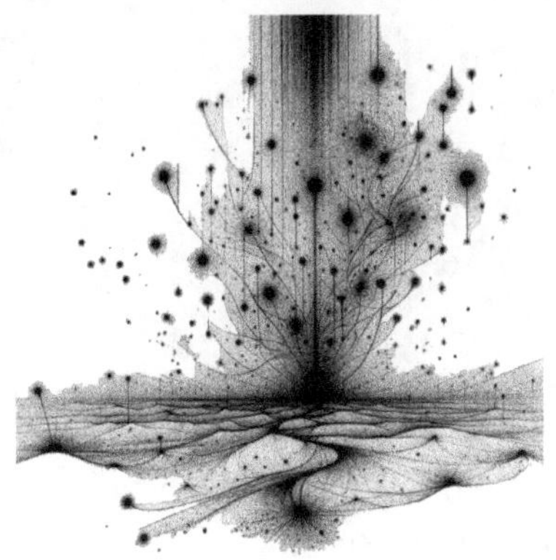

A sunbeam breaks through the veil of clouds,
Illuminating dirt and dust.
Reminding me that even the smallest particles
dance in the light.

As the sunlight shifts, its impression remains.
A snapshot of simple beauty,
Embedded in my mind.

And this is a lesson from dirt and dust.
That brilliance is not only found in the stars.
Even the humblest forms can catch the light and
become radiant.

Never Be

Heart stops
She beats no further
Just trembling and shaking
Nothing left remains.

Hollowed-out empty chambers
once filled with vibrant life
Love flowed freely once
But it will never be again.
It can never be again.

Time

Time plays a cruel game
It promises healed wounds
While ripping away the scabs,
Exposing memories long forgotten

There is no filling of the gaps
Just the gaping holes that you left
No surgical tape to fix
The fractured pieces of my heart

How do I move on when there is nowhere to go?
Can we go back to the day before yesterday?

Find You in the Chaos

Words could not express
the empty pages of my heart.
I tried to sing you a new song;
I just never knew where to start.
Maybe in the silence
among the ashes of my soul
I'll find you in the chaos
where I let my passions go.

My Voice No Longer Sings

My voice no longer sings,
A muted violin in a forgotten symphony.
The notes are there, written on the air,
But they vanish, petals in a windstorm,
Unheard.

I strum the strings of my guitar,
But the melody is a ghost,
Fading before it forms,
A love song with no lover,
A psalm with no choir.

The words I penned,
Once drenched in hues of passion and fire,
Now ash-gray, dissolving at the edges,
The ink of my soul running dry,
An empty well in a barren land.

I search for God,
The Healer of wounds, mender of broken
chords,
And in the silence, I find, not emptiness,
But a space, a pause,
A breath between acts.

For though my voice no longer sings,

In the quiet, I hear a whisper,
A nudge toward rebirth,
The silent inkling that my story,
My song is far from over.
And in that stillness,
I find the tune I thought I'd lost,
Humble and soft,
Yet profoundly, undeniably,
Mine.

Within These Walls

Within these walls,
I found my voice,
She echoes that,
she made the right choice.
To sing of love, of loss, of pain,
In verses that, my heart still sustains.

It's here that my heart,
learned to roam,
In this vast,
and internal home.
My journey deep,
where shadows play,
In halls of night,
in dreams of day.

I walk these halls daily,
and ever more,
Because each step leads me,
to something more.
It's my path to heal,
to be set free,
From all of the lies,
that imprisoned me.

Rising After Failure

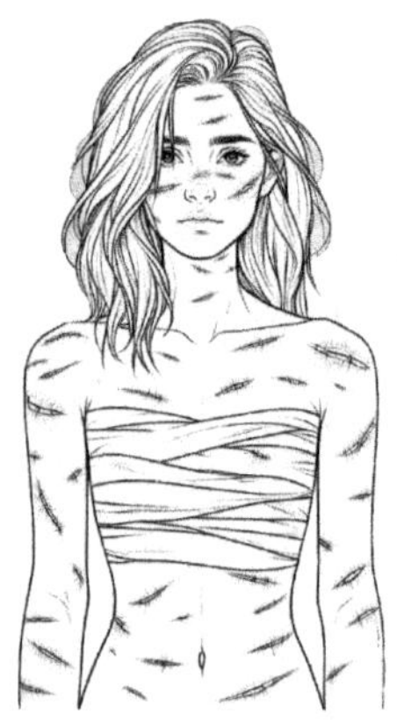

In the dark valley of defeat,
Where my dreams lay broken,
hope retreats.
I hear a voice call out my name,
Igniting once again,
this extinguished flame.

I am fallen, but not undone,
My journey's end has not yet come,
With scraped knees and a heavy heart,
I'll rise again to play my part.

Failure's grip may wound my pride,
But in those wounds, my strength resides,
For every scar and every tear,

Forges the path that has brought me here.

I'll stand again and with courage face,
The winding road, life's arduous race,
For in the stumble, truth I'll find,
Resilience, that is, my heart's true sign.

I'll Embrace the fall yet rise once more,
Stronger than I was before,
For failure is merely a hidden guide,
On the path to the other side.

I Will Rise

In the fire, truth is revealed.
My heart and spirit,
tempered and sealed.

I may be marked, but I'm not alone.
With every struggle, my resolve has grown.
And from the ashes
I WILL RISE.

Release

I learned to dance with my shadow,
as I sang her lullabies.
I became acquainted with the sound of grief,
releasing all her cries.

In the Quiet

In the quiet.
In the storm.
In all the spaces in between.
I found a shape.
I found a girl.
Who spent her life unseen.

Grieve It All

In the silence deep within,
Grieve it all.
Each fragment of joy, each shard of pain,
Unveil it! Unmask it!
Silence feigned indifference!

Do not pretend that you're ok!
For in the rawness of your soul's cry,
Lies the truth of your journey,
A path etched in the sands of what is real.

Refuse to bury your sorrows
in a dark corner of your heart.
Don't let them grow unacknowledged.
Turning joy into a shadow
and love into a ghost.

It was real, as real as the tears that fell.
Unbidden, in the stillness of night.
The love I experienced – a radiant flame,
Illuminating the deepest caverns of my being.

It was real in every laugh, in every touch,
In the whispered promises of dawn,
And in the aching silence of dusk.
It was real in its fleeting, ephemeral beauty.
I grieve, not in silence, but in poetry,
In songs that echo the rhythms of my heart.
For in the very act of grieving,
Lies the balm that heals, the love that liberates.

I won't shy away from this sacred pain.
For it bears witness to the love I've known.
A witness to the depths that I would go,
To connect with the one I held so close to my
heart.

I will grieve it all.
And I will find the strength to love again.
Brighter, bolder, with heart and hands wide
open.
Embracing it all.
The joy.
The pain.
The real.

Twenty Twenty-Three

This was the year it all came crashing down.
The year that I realized my heart had not been
found.
All of my dreams, scattered in the wind
But even in the chaos, a new journey did begin.

Now, standing in the ashes of all I thought I
knew
I find beauty so rare and so fiercely true.
All these shattered pieces, lessons in disguise
Teaching me resilience, teaching me to cry.

In the heart of this storm, I found my voice
Whispering of hope amidst the deafening noise.
Through the cracks of broken dreams, I can still
see
The light of His love shining down on me.

Twenty twenty-three, the year of my undoing
Became the year of my soul's renewing.
For in the soil of my heart, I planted seeds of
new dreams
Watered by tears and the moon's gentle beams.

I stand here broken but stronger in strife
Carving a path in my canvas of life.

With each step, I weave a tale of rebirth
My story of resilience and my precious life's
worth.

So here's to the year that taught me to fall
And rise like a phoenix, high above it all.
For in the art of falling, I learned to fly
This was the year I discovered my battle cry.

In the Light of Your Love

In the light of Your love
My path was so clear
Through forests of doubt
Your warmth drew me near.
And in shadows that danced
Your radiance shone
Guiding my steps
In a world once unknown.

In the light of Your love
The stars whispered tales
Of my destiny's journey
Where my courage prevails.
The moon sang in harmony
With my soul's song
In the light of Your love
I truly belong.

In dark storms of fear
Your light was my shield
A beacon of hope
In the darkness revealed.
With each ray of Your love
My spirit took flight
In the light of Your love
All my world felt right.

In the heart of your light
I discovered my home
Where You brought me to life
Where I'm never alone.
In the light of Your love
Life's symphony plays
A song of sweet joy
That sets my heart ablaze.

Beautiful

You know my name
You see the scars that keep
me hidden in dark places

You know my shame
You see the wounds I try to hide
in the inner parts of me

Yet you call me beautiful.

Transformed

Piece by piece.
I solved the puzzle.
My frame was finally formed.
From the dark.
Into the light.
My soul has been transformed.